People and Buildings

LOCAL STUDIES
IN HISTORY AND
GEOGRAPHY

Rosemary Rees

Janet Withersby

Heinemann

First published in Great Britain by Heinemann Library, Halley Court, Jordan Hill, Oxford OX2 8EJ
a division of Reed Educational and Professional Publishing Ltd

OXFORD FLORENCE PRAGUE MADRID ATHENS MELBOURNE AUCKLAND KUALA LUMPUR
SINGAPORE TOKYO IBADAN NAIROBI KAMPALA JOHANNESBURG GABORONE
PORTSMOUTH NH CHICAGO MEXICO CITY SAO PAULO

Designed by Aricot Vert Design

Illustrations by Melanie Jones

Originated in the UK by Dot Gradations Ltd, Wickford

Printed in the UK by Jarrold Book Printing Ltd, Thetford

00 99 98 97 96

10 9 8 7 6 5 4 3 2 1

ISBN 0 431 07891 2

British Library Cataloguing in Publication Data

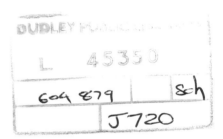

Rees, Rosemary, 1942 –

   People and buildings – (Local studies in history and geography)
   1. Buildings – Juvenile literature **2. Dwellings** – Juvenile literature
   I. Title II. Withersby, Janet
   643.1

Acknowledgements

The Publishers would like to thank the following for permission to reproduce photographs:
ACE: p.4; ARCAID/David Fowler: p.4; Burnley Borough Council, Graphics Unit: p.24; Lancashire Library: p.26;
Leeds City Library: p.16; Oxfordshire Photographic Archives, DLA OCC: p.7;
Roger Scruton: pp: 3, 6, 8-13, 17, 20-23, 25, 27-29; Kate Vaughan Williams: pp.14-15;
Janet Withersby: p.11

Cover photograph reproduced with permission of Collections, G. Peacock.

Maps reproduced from Ordnance Survey mapping with the permission of The Controller
of Her Majesty's Stationery Office © Crown Copyright, Licence No. MC8575 OM.

Our thanks to Jane Shuter for her comments in the preparation of this book.

Every effort has been made to contact copyright holders of any material reproduced in this book.
Any omissions will be rectified in subsequent printings if notice is given to the Publisher.

Contents

Houses: old and new   4

Building houses   6

Clues from houses   8

Recording   10

Schools: old and new   12

Barns: then and now   14

Churches: then and now   16

Clues from maps   18

A village: shops and school   20

A village: houses and church   22

Clues from town plans   24

Clues from photographs   26

A town: 19th-century houses   28

Glossary   30

Index   32

Houses: old and new

When was your house built?

Do you live in a house on a new estate? Do you live in a modern block of flats? Or do you live in an old cottage in a village? Perhaps you live in an old house in the middle of a town. Whatever your house is like, it was built by someone. It may have been built by Tudor craftsmen, **Victorian** bricklayers or modern construction workers.

Old or new?

To find out the age of a house, first of all look carefully at the house itself. The design of the house might give you a clue. Modern houses have large doors and windows. Some of them have garages. Older houses might have uneven roofs and tall chimneys.

They might have windows made up of lots of small **panes**. You might find some very old trees in the garden. Look at houses that are being built today. Compare them with a house you think is older, and try to work out what is different.

*The cottage with the **thatched** roof (above) was built in Worcestershire in about 1550. The stone cottage (left), was built in Yorkshire in about 1700.*

These datestones tell us the ages of the buildings.

Memories

Perhaps you can remember your house or flat being built. Adults who have lived in the same place for a long time can sometimes remember when houses, and even whole streets of houses, were built or knocked down.

Datestones

It is sometimes difficult to date old houses. This is because people built using the same materials for hundreds of years. They were materials that were found locally. But **datestones** can help us.

Sometimes the first owner of a house was so proud of the house that he or she wanted a datestone put on it. A **stonemason** chiselled the date on which the building was finished on a special block of stone. The builder then put this datestone over a window or doorway.

If you are lucky enough to find a datestone, you can find out more by looking at old maps made around the same time. These should show you what the town or village was like before your house was put up, and what it was like afterwards.

Look very carefully at the houses you see. Try to work out if they are new or old.

LOOK OUT

Sometimes, when really old buildings were rebuilt, the datestones were moved. Look for datestones in odd places

Building houses

What is your home built from?

Do you live in a block of flats built from **steel** and **concrete**? Do you live in a house built from bricks? Or do you live in an old cottage built from stone? If your home is new, the builders may have ordered the bricks, steel, concrete and plastic from factories far away. Lorries will have brought all these materials to the people who were building your home.

These are some houses in Kenton, a town in Devon. They were built in the 1870s from red bricks. Can you spot the patterns? The builders made the patterns from lighter coloured bricks.

Local materials

In the past it was different. There were no lorries travelling down motorways, taking building materials to wherever they were needed. People built their homes from the materials that were close at hand. They built them from **sandstone** and **limestone**, wood and blocks of turf. In some places people built houses by putting up a strong frame made from thick pieces of wood. The walls in-between were made from thin branches and twigs, plastered with mud. This is called **wattle and daub**. In other parts of the country people built their houses from **clunch**, which is a mixture of mud and **flints**.

Look at the houses in the picture. How could you find out whether or not they were built from local materials?

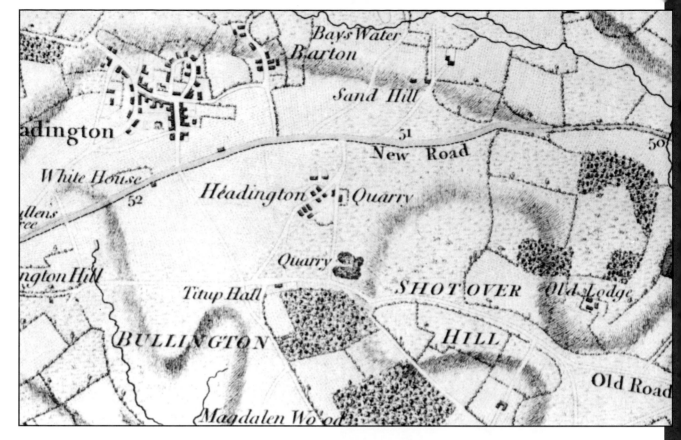

This is a map of a part of Headington, a town in Oxfordshire. The map was made in 1797.

Clues from maps

If you think that a house is made from local materials, you could try to check if this is right. If the house was built with bricks, first look to see whether there are more houses in the street built from the same sort of bricks. This might be a clue that the bricks were made locally. Next, look at a map that was made at about the same time as the house was built. If you can find a **brickworks** on the map, then it is very likely the houses were built from local bricks. In order to be really sure, you would need to find out what sort of bricks were made in the brickworks and compare them with the bricks in the houses.

Look at the map on this page. Look for the quarry. Stone comes from quarries. What does this tell you about the building materials that might have been used here? Look at the roads. Where does Old Road go? Why do you think New Road was built?

LOOK OUT

Sometimes modern builders build houses in a special way so that they look old, not new. See if you can spot any houses like this.

Clues from houses

What can you see?

Look very carefully at the outside of old houses. You can find interesting clues as to what the inside of a house used to be like. The way houses have been changed sometimes tells us about what was happening in Britain.

This is a photograph of an old house in Burnley, Lancashire. Look carefully and you can see that an opening has been blocked up. What do you think the opening was once used for?

Blocked up doors and windows

If you look at some old houses, you may be able to spot blocked up doors and windows. You may see a door **lintel**, but with a stone wall underneath it and no door. You may see window **mullions**, but no windows, only a wall. Why did people make these changes?

Changing rooms around

Sometimes people blocked up doors and windows because they decided to change the ways in which the rooms were organized inside the house. Perhaps they wanted to block off a door to make a room larger, or knock a door through to somewhere else. Some houses had cow sheds attached. When the owner became rich, he moved the cows into a separate **shippon**, and turned the old shed into a new room.

Government taxes

Sometimes windows were blocked up for other reasons. After 1792, people who owned houses with between seven and nine windows had to pay two **shillings** in **tax** to the government. Houses with between ten and nineteen windows were taxed at four shillings. People who wanted to pay less tax blocked up some of their windows.

Roofs and chimneys

Look at chimneys. Sometimes there is one chimney pot for each **grate** in a house. This will tell you how many fireplaces there were in the house. Sometimes there were fireplaces in the bedrooms as well as in the main rooms of the house. Some older houses have been **modernized**. Their owners have had central heating put in. Central heating needs a different sort of chimney.

Look at the photograph of chimneys on this page. What do they tell you about the ways in which the different houses are heated?

This is a photograph of houses with different chimneys in Preston, a town in Lancashire. How were the different houses heated?

LOOK OUT

Watch out for blocked-up openings in other sorts of old buildings. See how many you can spot.

9

Recording

Why is recording important?

When you find out something interesting about the past, you want to remember it. Other people will want to know about it. This is why you must **record** what you have found out. You don't have to write it all down. You could make drawings. You could also save information on a computer disk, or you could record what you have found out on a cassette.

The children making their time-line.

Making a time-line

Look at the photograph. Jyoti, Mark, Dean, Kelly, Rebecca and Satveer are making a time-line. It is a big time-line, so they are making it in their school playground! Each of them has a photograph of a house. They have worked out when each house was built. They are putting the houses in date order on their time-line. Each house is underneath the date on which it was built. When their time-line is finished, all the children in their class will be able to see how houses have changed over time.

Making drawings

When you are looking at chimneys and doors, windows and walls, it is a good idea to make a quick drawing of what you see. Remember to label the different parts of your drawing. In that way you will remember the colours and shapes, and which parts were made of wood or stone.

Using a computer

Is there a computer you can use? Some computers have databases. A database can be used to store information. This information can then be sorted in different ways. You could **input** details of houses, for example, and then sort them into houses with **thatched** roofs and houses with tiled roofs. In this way you could see the ways in which building materials have changed over time.

number
of windows

window
shape

colour

lintel
shape

brick
pattern

materials
glass
stone
brick
wood

Kelly and Jyoti are using a computer to sort out information about houses.

Some children collected and recorded information about Victorian houses by making pencil drawings. They used their information to make paintings like this when they got back to school.

LOOK OUT

Record as much detail as you can while you are out and about. Later, you can always ignore what you do not want, but you might not always be able to go back and have another look!

Schools: old and new

What does your school look like?

Do you go to a modern school with large windows, and walls built from concrete panels? Or is your school an old one, built with bricks, and does it have windows high up in the walls? Perhaps your school has a **foundation stone** or a datestone so that you know when it was built. Your school may have been built over a hundred years ago, but perhaps it has modern classrooms built on to it.

This is a modern photograph of a Victorian school. The school is in Pickering, North Yorkshire.

What did Victorian schools look like?

Many children today go to schools that were built in **Victorian** times. Victorian schools often had windows that were too high for children to look out of. Victorian teachers were afraid that, if the windows were lower, their pupils would spend too long watching what was going on outside and would not pay attention to their lessons. Victorian schools had separate entrances for boys and girls, and separate playgrounds as well. Teachers did not want boys and girls to mix too much once they had left the Infants.

Making old schools bigger

Look at the photograph on this page. Can you see the old school? This is now part of a larger school. Can you spot the new building? How do you know it is newer than the old building?

Why have old schools been made bigger?

Most old school buildings have modern **extensions**. These may be **temporary** classrooms. A lorry will have delivered them to the old school. The new classrooms will be taken away when they are no longer needed. Some new classrooms will be **permanent**. They are built from brick or stone and are usually joined on to the old school. All these extensions make more space in the school. The head teacher may have needed more classrooms because more children were joining the school. Maybe the school needed a new Hall or a new gym. The running of the school may have been getting more complicated, so that the head teacher needed more space for a bigger office.

This is the same school as the one in the photograph opposite. Can you spot the new extension? How do you know it is newer than the old school?

LOOK OUT

Find an old school with a new extension. What is the extension used for?

Barns: then and now

What do old barns look like?

Barns used to be made from stone, wood or bricks. Farmers built their barns in their farmyard and in corners of fields. Barns had to be strong enough to keep the wind and rain out. The barn doors had to be large enough for a horse and cart to get inside to deliver a load or load up.

What did farmers use barns for?

In the past, farmers used barns for storing the grain they had grown. When they **harvested** their wheat, barley, rye or oats they kept the sacks of grain in their barns. When the time was right, they took the grain to market to sell.

Not all farmers grew grain — some kept sheep and cows. Sheep and cows ate grass in the summer, but in the winter the grass was poor and they needed extra food. The farmers used their barns for storing hay which they fed to the animals in winter.

Sometimes farmers kept **ploughs** and other machinery in their barns. Animals were usually kept in other buildings. Sheep were kept in **shielings** or sheep-pens; cows were kept in **byres** or **shippons**.

This is a modern photograph of an old stone barn in Yorkshire. The barn was built in the 1850s. The farmer who owned the barn did not need it any more. The barn began to fall down.

Special barns

Tithe barns were special barns. They belonged to the Church. Until about 150 years ago, every person had to give to the Church one tenth of what he or she produced. This was called a tithe and was a sort of tax. The Church had to store all this somewhere, and so church people had enormous barns built. All the farmers in one **parish** delivered their tithes to the church's tithe barn.

Why don't modern farmers need old barns?

Modern farmers don't need to store grain in barns. They have specially built **grain silos** which keep the grain at exactly the right temperature and stop it from going mouldy. Modern farmers store winter hay and **silage** in huge black polythene sacks, not in barns.

In the past, barns were built to take a horse and cart. Modern equipment, like a **combine harvester**, is much too large to go in old barns. The church no longer collects tithes. So, all over Britain there are barns which are not used any more.

This is the same barn as the one in the photograph opposite. It has been rebuilt as a home.

LOOK OUT

Old barns have special openings in their walls to let air in so that the grain keeps dry. See if you can spot these openings.
All old barns have an owl hole at the very top of the side wall, just under the roof.
This was to let owls fly in and out. Why were owls good friends to farmers?

Churches: then and now

What are churches used for nowadays?

Churches are used by Christians. They go to church, usually on a Sunday, to worship. Christians often get married in church. They take their babies to church to be **baptized**. When they die, Christians have a funeral service in church, and are sometimes buried in the church **graveyard**.

What were churches used for in the past?

Churches were used for all these things, and more. Four hundred years ago, the church was one of the most important buildings in a **parish**.

People held markets and fairs inside the church. They gave one tenth of everything they made or earned to the Church.

The parish **priest** kept **registers**. In these registers he wrote the names of all the babies born in the parish, and who their parents were. He wrote down the names of the people who married in his church, and the names of those he buried. Often, this is the only record we have that these people ever existed. The priest had to keep the registers in a special parish chest.

This church was built in Leeds in 1905.

Why are some churches not needed any more?

Fewer church buildings are needed nowadays. There are many reasons for this. One reason is that fewer people are Christians than in the past, and so they do not need so many churches. In the 19th century more and more people moved into towns. Churches were built for them in the middle of growing towns and cities like Bradford, Birmingham and Leeds. Now people have moved out of the middle of towns. Some churches are not needed any more.

What happens to churches that are no longer needed?

A church may be pulled down when it is not needed any more. The land on which it stood is sold to be changed into a car park or perhaps a supermarket. Sometimes churches are sold and the new owners change them into offices, art galleries, shops or restaurants.

This is the same church as the one in the picture opposite. It is now a carpet shop.

LOOK OUT

See if you can spot a church that is being used for something else. What is it being used for?

Clues from maps

What can a map tell us?

There are lots of different sorts of maps. Some maps are of countries and show us where there are rivers, forests and mountains. Some maps of countries show us the **political boundaries** between different states and countries. They also show us the capital cities, state boundaries and main **ports**.

Scale

The **scale** of a map is important. The scale tells us the size of the map when it is compared to the real cities, rivers and mountains which the map shows. So a scale of 1:250 means that every centimetre on the map is 250 centimetres on the ground.

What can modern maps tell us about buildings?

Large-scale maps can show us the buildings in a village or town. Look at the map on this page. The village in the middle is called Colyton. It is in Devon. Find the church, the Post Office, the cemetery, the weir, the school, the railway and the station. What do they tell you about Colyton?

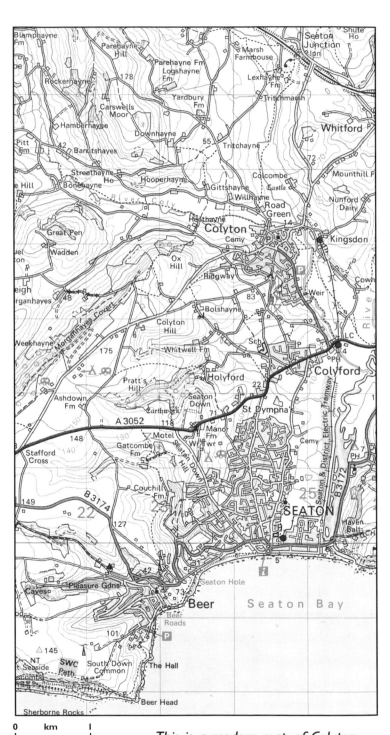

This is a modern map of Colyton and the area around the village.

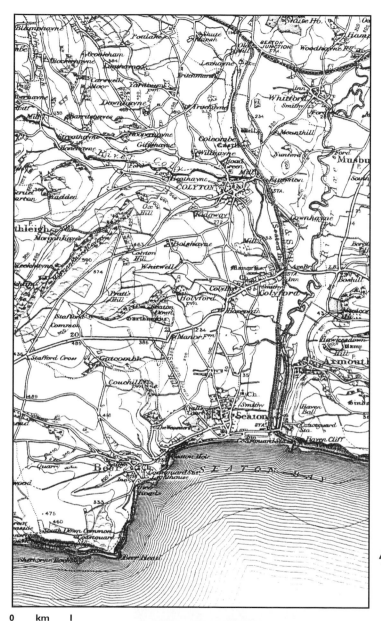

0   km   I

This map of Colyton and the surrounding area was made in 1892.

What can old maps tell us about buildings?

Old maps can give us the same sort of information as modern maps. Look carefully at the map of Colyton on this page. The map was made in 1892, over one hundred years ago. Find the church, the **mill**, the station and the railway line.

Comparing maps

We can learn even more if we compare two maps which were made at different times. What can you find on the 1992 map that is not on the map made in 1892? What can you find on the map of 1892 that is not on the 1992 map? What is the same on both maps? What does this tell you about the ways in which Colyton has changed over a hundred years?

LOOK OUT

All maps have scales. The size of the scale depends on who the map is for.

Why do lorry drivers use small scale maps and walkers use large scale maps?

A village: shops and school

Shops in a village

Village shops are usually small, and there are not many shops to choose from. Each shop will probably sell one or two sorts of goods. A greengrocer's shop sells fruit and vegetables. A butcher sells pieces of meat, and sausages. If you want baked beans or fish fingers, you will have to go to the grocer's shop.

Some villages have a garage that sells petrol and some have dress shops. If people want to buy furniture, a car or some books, they will probably have to travel by car or bus to the nearest town.

A village market

Until about a hundred years ago, most villagers shopped in the local market. People came to the village from farms and cottages in the countryside to buy and to sell. They sold all kinds of things: apples and green beans, fish and bacon, baskets and geese, eggs and cheese. They set up stalls in the market square and sold their goods there.

In larger villages there would be a market every day. In smaller villages, people set up markets every two or three days. Some villages still have markets, but they have shops as well.

These shops are in the village of Colyton in Devon.

This is the primary school in Colyton in Devon. It was built over a hundred years ago.

Village schools in the past

A hundred years ago most villages had their own school. In 1880 Parliament passed a law which said that all children had to go to school until they were ten years old. This meant that a lot of schools had to be built. Try to find out when the village school nearest to you was built.

Village schools today

Nowadays only really large villages have primary schools. Children from small villages and farms travel to them by bus, minibus or taxi. This is because it would cost too much money to have schools in villages were there are only five or six children.

LOOK OUT

Nowadays, not all villages have schools or markets. Look out for street names like 'School Lane' and 'Market Street'.
They will tell you that the village once had a school and a market.

A village: houses and church

Why do people live in villages nowadays?

Many people live in villages because they work there. They work in shops and pubs; they work in the doctor's surgery or the school. Other people live in villages because they like living in the countryside. They live there, but they work in nearby towns. They **commute** to town every day. Some people live and work in towns, but go to their village homes to relax at weekends. Other people who own houses in villages do not live there at all. They **let** their houses to people on holiday.

What kind of houses do they live in?

Some people live in new estates that are built on the edges of villages. The houses are modern – they are light, airy and easy to run. Other people live in older houses or cottages which are closer to the middle of the village. Some may not have been changed much since the time they were built. Sometimes the people living in them have **modernized** the cottages. The people who built the cottages would not recognize them now!

These old cottages are in Colyton in Devon. They have been painted outside and modernized inside by their owners.

Village churches

Nearly every village has a church. Some churches have square towers, and some have tall **steeples**. Some churches were built over a thousand years ago, when the Saxons were living in England.

This is the church in the village of Colyton in Devon. Look at the picture and try to work out whether Colyton was a rich or poor village when the church was built.

Graveyards

Most village churches have **graveyards** around them where people from the village are buried. The **gravestones** give us interesting information.

Some families have lived in the same village for hundreds of years. You can work this out from their names on gravestones in the graveyard. Some families had a lot of children and many of the children died when they were very young. This happened often in the past. Gravestones can tell you which were the bad years for a village, when there were illnesses from which many people died.

LOOK OUT

Some gravestones tell us about the work the dead person did when they were alive; some tell us, in an epitaph, what the dead person was like.

Clues from town plans

Town plans

When you visit a town for the first time, a sensible thing to do is to buy a town plan. You will be able to work out on the plan just where you are. You can plan a route to where you want to go. You will be able to work out how to get to the shops and the park, the cinema and the town hall. You will see where the roads go, and if there is a railway, bus station or canal.

Working people

A modern town plan can give you some clues about people. Shops, offices and factories all have people working in them. How do these people get to work? Check your town plan. Can you find car parks? Are the bus stops and bus routes marked on the map? Is there a railway station? All these will give you clues about how people get to work.

This is a plan of part of Burnley in Lancashire. What does the plan tell you about the town?

KEY

1   Town hall
2   Tourist information
3   Police station
4   Bus station
5   Shopping centre
6   Recreation centre
7   Library
8   Post office
P   Parking
▼   Toilet

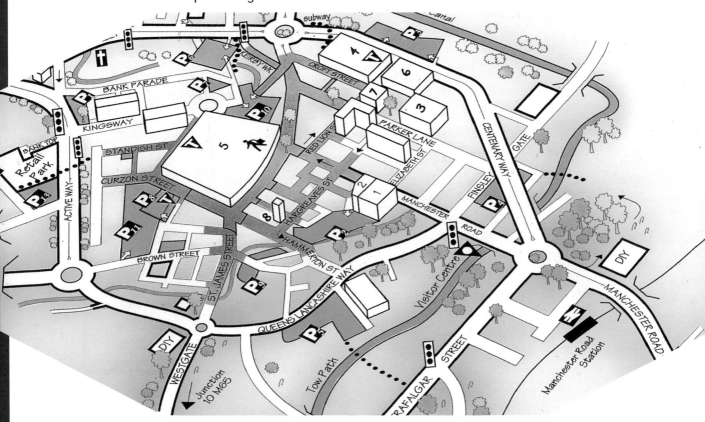

People at home

Some town plans will have houses on them. The houses may be built near the middle of the town. Do you think these are likely to be old or new houses? How could you check? The houses might be on estates on the outskirts of the town. Do you think these are likely to be old or new houses? Look to see whether the houses are close to schools and **clinics**. An estate of houses, with a school, would probably have been built since about 1930.

Not what they seem!

Not all plans tell you what is really there. Work out where the **toll house** is on the plan. Look at the photograph on this page. You will see that the old toll house has been turned into a museum, called a Visitor Centre.

The old toll house by the canal in Burnley, Lancashire, which is now a museum.

LOOK OUT

Look out for old industrial buildings that are now being used for something else.

Clues from photographs

Clues from photographs

Look carefully at the old photograph on this page. It was taken in Burnley, Lancashire, in 1870. It can tell us a lot about towns at this time, and something about the people who lived there.

This photograph of the church in Burnley, Lancashire, was taken in 1870.

Roads and railings

The road outside the church is made from **cobbles** and it is very wide. This means it had a lot of **traffic** on it. Find out what sort of traffic there would have been in 1870. It must have been an important road. How can you find out where it went?

The railings outside the church, and round the building next to the church, are made from iron. What does this tell us about **industry** at that time?

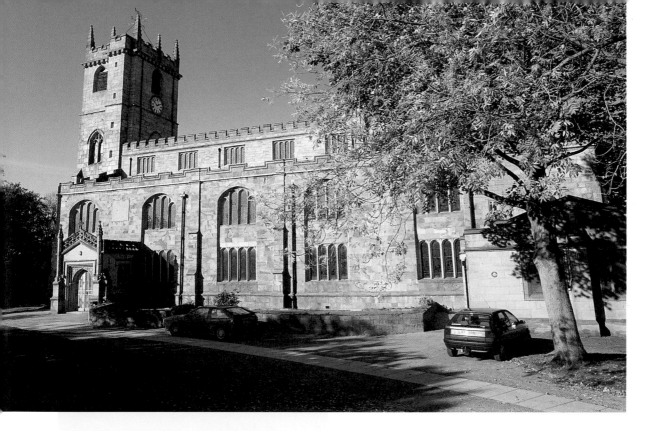

This photograph of the church in Burnley was taken in 1996.

People in photographs

Look at the people in the old photograph. Are they poor people, rich people or people who are neither rich nor poor? How can you tell? Do you think they just happened to be walking past the church when the photograph was taken? Or are they standing there specially for the photograph? Why do you think the photograph was taken? Was it taken as a photograph of the people or the church?

It is usually quite easy to work out who people are in old family photographs. Why would it be difficult to find out who these people were?

Clues from modern photographs

The photograph on this page was taken in 1996. It is of the same church in Burnley. What differences can you spot between this photograph and the old photograph? If you make a list of the differences you will be able to work out some of the changes that happened in Burnley between 1870 and 1996.

LOOK OUT

Find an old photograph of the place you live in. Then try to work out what has changed between the time the photograph was taken and now.

A town: 19th-century houses

Industrial towns in the 19th century

Many towns grew very quickly in the 19th century. New factories, **mills** and all kinds of businesses were opening. Burnley, in Lancashire, was one of these towns. The main **industry** in Burnley was cotton **spinning** and **weaving**. More and more cotton mills were built. They needed people to work in them. These people needed houses to live in.

Houses in industrial towns

During the 19th century, thousands and thousands of new homes for workers were built quickly and cheaply. Builders built them in long terraces and round square courtyards.

These terrace houses were built in Burnley in the 19th century.

Some builders built 'back-to-back' houses. These shared side walls and a back wall as well.

Many houses in which poor people lived did not have any water piped to them until the end of the 19th century. Their lavatories were not connected up to sewers. Dirty, crowded conditions meant that diseases like **cholera** and **tuberculosis** spread very quickly. Local **town councils** and the government decided that they had to make sure that people lived in healthy conditions.

Rules and laws

From the 1860s, many town councils made rules about how new homes had to be built. The town council of Huddersfield, in West Yorkshire, said that no back-to-back houses could be built. In 1875 Parliament passed a Public Health Act. This said that town councils had to build sewers and run a clean water supply to all houses.

19th-century houses today

Some 19th-century houses were very badly built. Most of these have been pulled down. Some of them, however, were well built and have lasted until today. They have been **modernized** and are now lived in by all kinds of people with all kinds of jobs. People like them because they are usually close to the middle of towns. This means that people who live in them can get to work quickly, and go out in the evenings without having to make a long journey home.

These are the backs of the terrace houses in Burnley. How have they changed since they were built?

Glossary

baptize when a priest touches a person with holy water to show they belong to a church

brickworks a place where bricks are made

byre a cow shed

cholera a deadly disease carried in dirty water

clinic where people go to see a nurse or a doctor

clunch a mixture of mud and flints

cobbles round stones set in the ground to make a road or path

combine harvester machine for cutting and gathering grain

commute travel from home to work

concrete cement and stones mixed to make a hard building material

datestone a special stone, set in a house wall, showing the date when the house was built

extension something added on

flints hard stones

foundation stone a specially carved stone to mark the start of work on an important building

grain silo a tall tower holding grain

grate where a fire is lit in a house

gravestone a stone which shows where a person is buried

graveyard the ground around a church where people are buried

harvest gather in crops when they are ripe

industry work, usually with machinery

input putting information into a computer

key information which tells you what all the symbols on a map mean

let allow people to live in a house you own if they pay you money

limestone a type of rock

lintel a stone bar across the top of a door or window opening

mill a place where cotton is spun and woven

modernize bring an old house up-to-date

mullions upright blocks of stone dividing up a window

panes pieces of glass set in a window frame

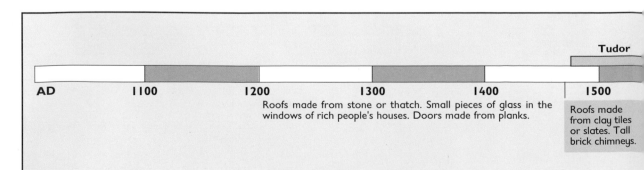

Tudor

AD   1100   1200   1300   1400   1500

Roofs made from stone or thatch. Small pieces of glass in the windows of rich people's houses. Doors made from planks.

Roofs made from clay tiles or slates. Tall brick chimneys.

parish an area run by the local church

permanent always there

plough a tool, pulled by a horse or a tractor, which turns the soil over

political boundaries lines on a map which show where one state or country ends and another begins

port a town or city with docks by the sea

priest a person who runs a church

record write down, draw or describe what you have found out

registers special books in which the priest wrote down every baptism, marriage and burial that happened in his church

sandstone a type of rock

scale the size of a map compared to the real place

shieling a sheep pen

shilling an old amount of money equal to 5p today

shippon a cowshed

silage winter food for animals

spinning turning raw cotton or wool into thread

steel a type of metal

steeple a tall, pointed top to a church tower

stonemason a person who is specially skilled in carving and shaping stone

tax money or goods taken from what a person earns or makes

temporary only there for a short time

thatch a roof made from rushes

tithe a church tax of one tenth of people's earnings

toll house where a toll keeper lived; the toll keeper collected money from people who wanted to use a road

town council a group of people who run a town

traffic vehicles on a road

tuberculosis a disease of the lungs

wattle and daub walls made from thin branches or twigs (wattle) plastered with mud (daub)

weaving turning thread into cloth

Victorians people who lived during the reign of Queen Victoria (1837–1901)

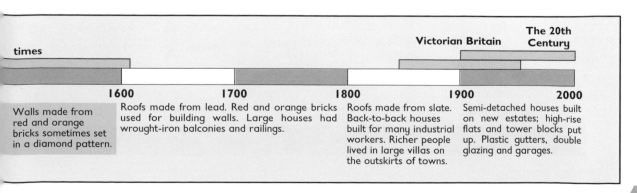

times

| 1600 | 1700 | 1800 | Victorian Britain 1900 | The 20th Century 2000 |

Walls made from red and orange bricks sometimes set in a diamond pattern.

Roofs made from lead. Red and orange bricks used for building walls. Large houses had wrought-iron balconies and railings.

Roofs made from slate. Back-to-back houses built for many industrial workers. Richer people lived in large villas on the outskirts of towns.

Semi-detached houses built on new estates; high-rise flats and tower blocks put up. Plastic gutters, double glazing and garages.

Index

Numbers in plain type (27) refer to the text. Numbers in italic type (27) refer to a caption or a picture.

animals 8, 14

back-to-back houses 28, 29
barns 14–15, *14, 15*
boundaries 18
bricks 6, *6*, 7, *11*, 13, 14
brickworks 7
building alterations 8–9, 13, *15*, 17, 22, *22*, 29, *29*
building materials 6–7, 11
Burnley *8, 24, 25, 26, 26, 27, 27*, 28, *28*, 29
byres 14

chimneys 4, 9, *9*
churches 16–17, *16, 17*, 23, 26, *26, 27, 27*
clunch 6
Colyton 18, *18*, 19, *19*, 20, 21, 22, 23
cottages 4, 22, *22*

datestones 5, 12
dating a house 4, 5
doors 4, 8

extensions 13, *13*

fireplaces 9
flats 4
foundation stones 12

grain silos 15
grates 9
gravestones 23
graveyards 16, 23

Headington 7
heating 9
houses 4–9, *6, 8, 9*, 10, 11, 25, 28, 29
    alterations 8–9, 22, *22*, 29, *29*
    building materials 6–7, 11
    cottages 4, 22, *22*
    dating a house 4, 5
    nineteenth-century houses 28–9
    terrace houses 29, *29*
housing estates 22, 25
Huddersfield 29

industry 25, 26, 28

Kenton 6

Leeds *16*
limestone 6
lintels 8, *11*

maps 5, 7, 18–19
    Colyton *18, 19*
    Headington 7
markets 20
mills 19, 28
mullions 8

owl holes 15

parish registers 16
photographs 26–7
Pickering *12*
Preston 9

quarries 7

recording information 10–11
roofs 4, 9

sandstone 6
schools 12–13, *12, 13*, 21, *21*
sewers 28, 29
shielings 14
shippons 8, 14
shops 20, *20*
silage 15
stone 7, *11*, 13, 14
stonemasons 5

taxes 8, 15, 16
terrace houses 29, *29*
thatch 4
tithe barns 15
tithes 15, 16
toll house 25, *25*
town plans 24–5
towns 17, 24–9

Victorian times 12, 26, 28–9
villages 20–3

water supply 28, 29
wattle and daub 6
window tax 8
windows 4, 8, *11*, 12
wood 6, *11*, 14